READ~ ALOUD BIBLE STORIES

VOL. 4

Ella K. Lindvall

ILLUSTRATED BY
H. Kent Puckett

MOODY PRESS
CHICAGO

j220-950
LIN

To
Scott, Laura, Michael, and Rileigh

And to Jason

Moody Press, a ministry of the Moody Bible Institute, is designed for education, evangelization, and edification. If we may assist you in knowing more about Christ and the Christian life, please write us without obligation: Moody Press, c/o MLM, Chicago, Illinois 60610.

17.99

Contents

Joseph and His Brothers
(Genesis 37:3-28; 39:1-5, 20-21;
41:39-40; 43:29-34; 45:16-20)

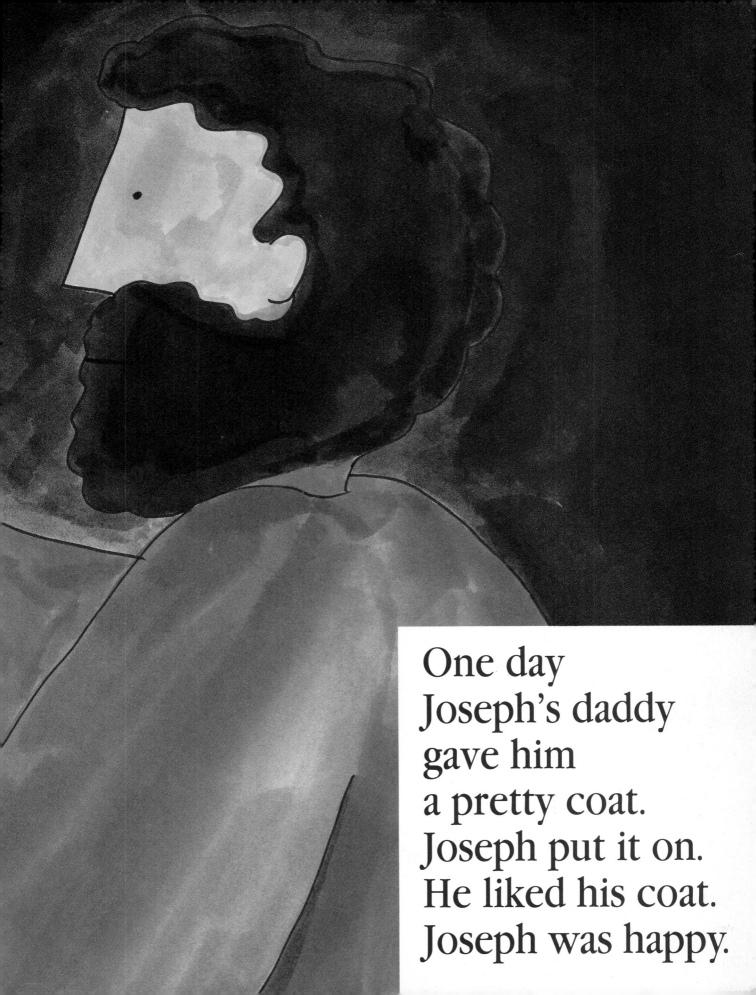

One day
Joseph's daddy
gave him
a pretty coat.
Joseph put it on.
He liked his coat.
Joseph was happy.

But Joseph's brothers were not happy.

On another day Joseph's brothers went to find some grass for the sheep.

Joseph's daddy said, "Joseph, please go and see if your brothers and the sheep are all right."

So Joseph put on
his pretty coat,
and *step, step, step,*
up the road he went
to find his brothers.
Joseph was happy.

Now the brothers saw Joseph coming. They saw his pretty coat. Joseph's brothers were not happy.

After a while,
clip, clop,
clip, clop,
some men came by
riding on camels.
And—oh, no!—
Joseph's brothers
let the men
take Joseph
away with them.

The men took Joseph
to a far-away place.
Was Joseph happy?
No, but God was there.
And God helped him.

In the far-away place,
Joseph worked
for a soldier.
Was Joseph happy?
No, but God was there.
And God helped him.

One day the soldier
put Joseph in jail.
Was Joseph happy?
No, but God was there.
And God helped him.

After a while
Joseph got to work
for the king.
Was Joseph happy?
No, but God was there.
And God helped him.

One day Joseph's brothers came.
They had not been nice to Joseph.
But now they were sorry.
Would Joseph be mean to them?
No, Joseph was kind.
He gave his brothers
something to eat.

The king said, "Joseph,
tell your daddy,
tell your brothers,
tell ALL your family
to come and live here,
close to you."
NOW do you think Joseph was happy?

What did you learn?

Some days are happy.
Some days are not happy.
But don't worry.
God is always with you.
He wants to help.

The Baby in the Basket
(Exodus 1:15-16; 2:1-10)

One day the bad king said, "I don't want any more boy babies. Take all the boy babies and throw them away."

Now this mommy
and this daddy
had a pretty baby boy.
They loved him.
Did they want
to throw him away?
Oh, no.

God told the mommy
what to do.
She made a little basket.
She put the baby
in the basket.
Then she hid the basket
with the baby inside.
Do you know
where she hid it?

She hid it
in the tall grass
beside the water.
Who would ever look
for a baby THERE?
Nobody.

The mommy said to Big Sister, "You stand here. You make sure NOBODY takes this basket."

Now the king—
remember him?—
the king had a big girl.
She was the princess.

One day the princess
went for a walk,
step, step, step.
Her helpers went with her,
step, step, step.
They all went walking
beside the water.

They walked up,
step, step, step.
They walked down,
step, step, step.
Then the princess
saw the basket.

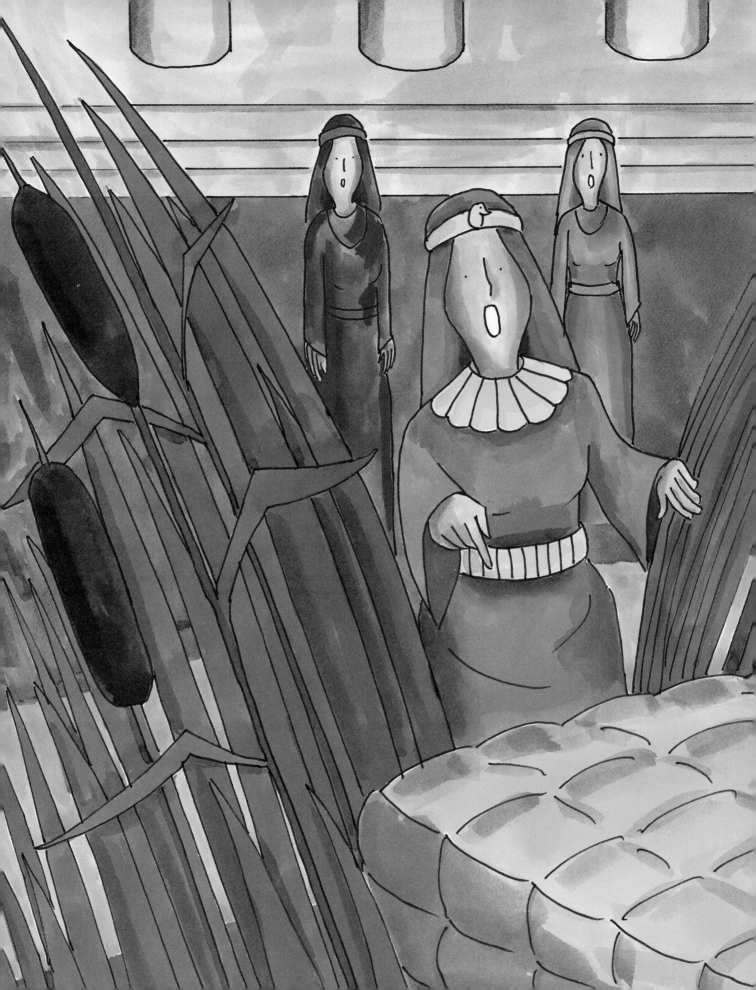

"What's THAT
in the grass?"
(*We* know what it was,
don't we?)
The princess said,
"Bring it here to me."
Oh, my!

One of her helpers
brought the basket.
The princess
looked inside and—
what's this?
A BABY BOY!
The baby started to cry.
"Oh," the princess said. "Oh."
(Do you think
she liked him?)

God told Big Sister
what to do.
Big Sister came fast.
Big Sister said,
"Shall I find somebody
to take care of the baby
for you?"
The princess said—

"Yes."
And off ran Big Sister.
(Go fast, Big Sister!
Go fast!)
Off ran Big Sister
to find the baby's mommy.

The princess said,
"Take care of this baby,
and I will give you pennies."
The mommy was happy.
She didn't care
about the pennies.
She just wanted her baby.
She picked him up,
and she took him home.

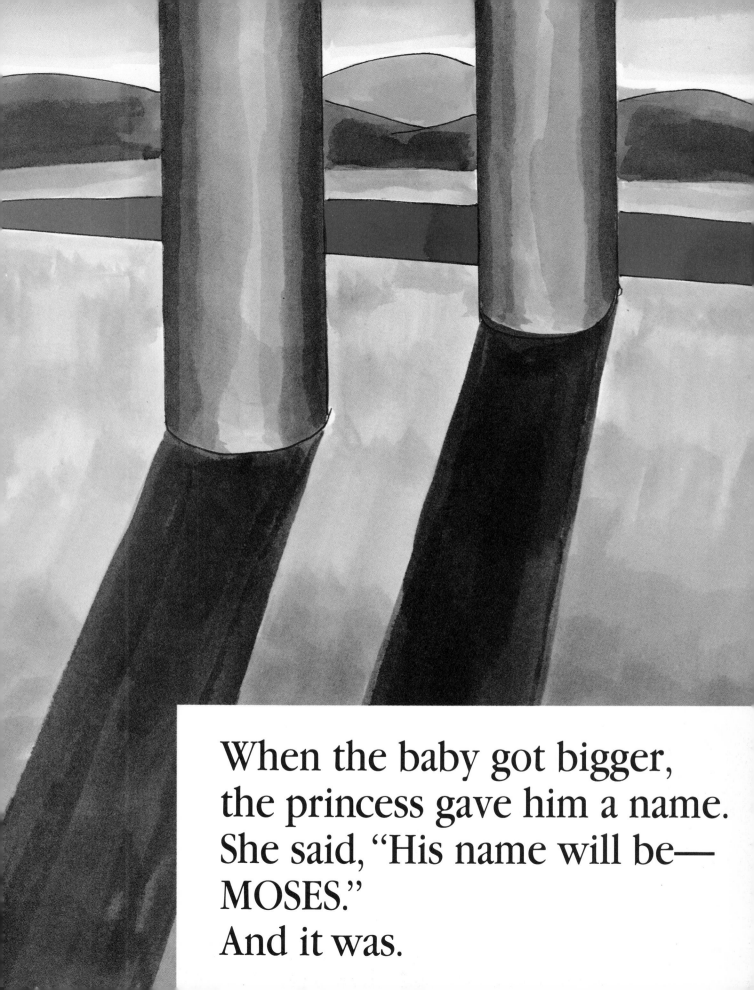

When the baby got bigger, the princess gave him a name. She said, "His name will be— MOSES." And it was.

What did you learn?

God told the mommy what to do. God told Big Sister what to do. God knew how to take care of baby Moses.

He knows how to take care of you too.

Joshua and the Big Wall
(Joshua 6:1-20)

Joshua was a man.
God told Joshua what to do.
Then Joshua told
God's people.

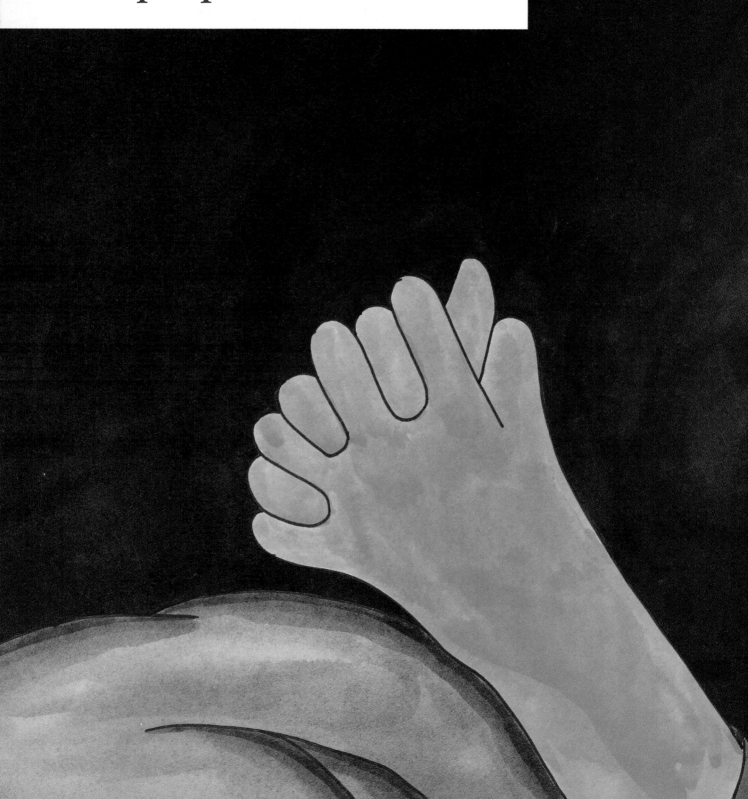

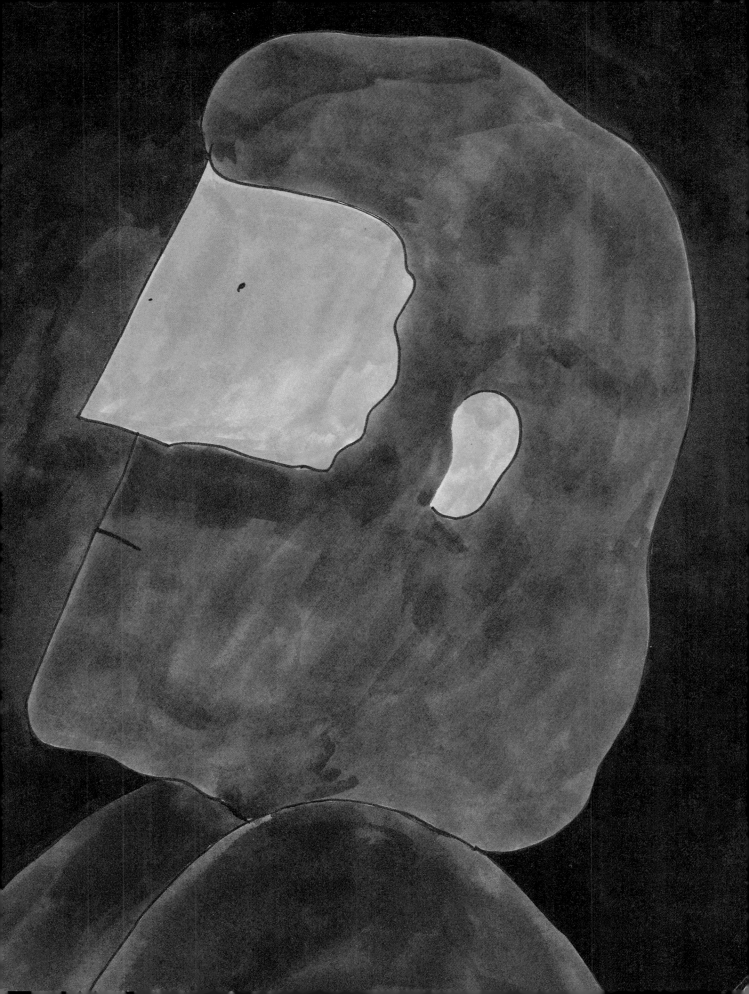

Jericho was a place.
Jericho had houses in it.
Jericho had a big wall
around it.

The big wall had a door.
Everyday the Jericho people
went in and out,
in and out,
in and out
their door.

Now God wanted *His* people inside Jericho.
But the Jericho people said no.
The Jericho people shut their door tight.

And their wall was SO BIG
that it kept everybody out.

God knew what to do.
God told Joshua.
And Joshua told God's people:
"Horn-blowers, line up!
Soldiers, line up!"

"Shhh," he said.
"Don't talk
until I tell you.
But horn-blowers,
you get ready
to blow your horns."

Then away went the soldiers,
away went the horn-blowers,
step, step, step, step,
on their way to Jericho.

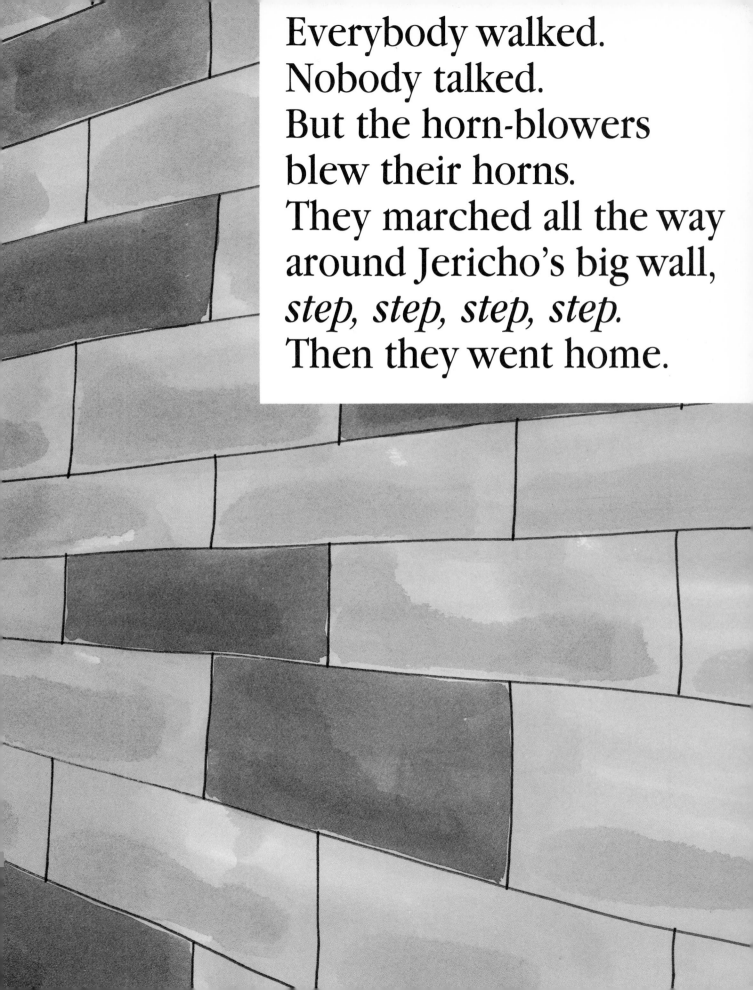

Everybody walked.
Nobody talked.
But the horn-blowers
blew their horns.
They marched all the way
around Jericho's big wall,
step, step, step, step.
Then they went home.

The next day
they marched around again,
step, step, step, step.
Everybody walked.
Nobody talked.
But the horn-blowers
blew their horns.

The next day—
guess what.
They went again.
And the next day,
and the next . . .
around and around,
step, step, step, step.
Everybody walked.
Nobody talked.
But the horn-blowers
blew their horns.

And then Joshua said, "NOW!"

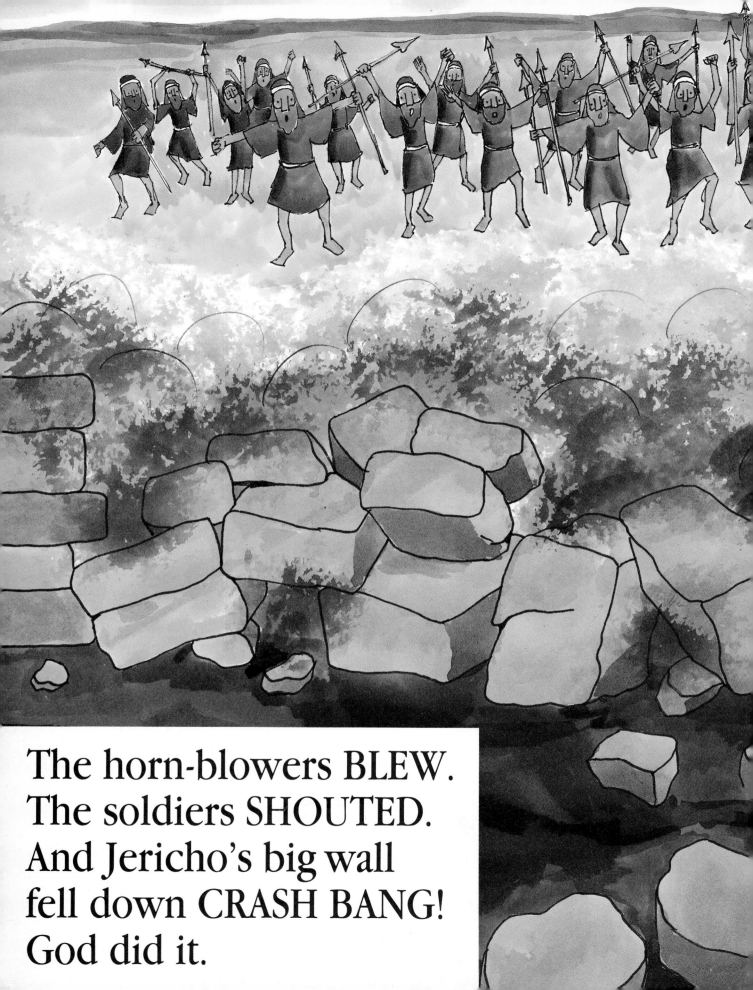

The horn-blowers BLEW.
The soldiers SHOUTED.
And Jericho's big wall
fell down CRASH BANG!
God did it.

And God's people walked
right into Jericho.
They didn't even need the door.

What did you learn?

Joshua obeyed.
He did what God said.
God's people obeyed.
They did what Joshua said.
Who should you obey?
Who else?

David and the Biggest Man
(1 Samuel 17:1-11, 34-58)

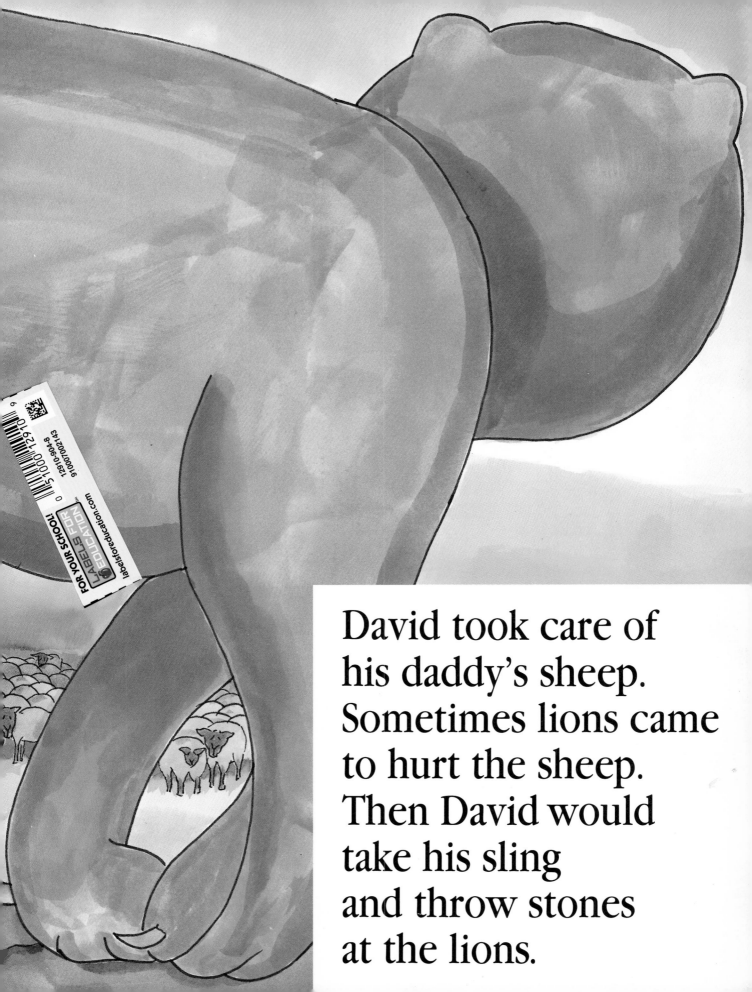

David took care of
his daddy's sheep.
Sometimes lions came
to hurt the sheep.
Then David would
take his sling
and throw stones
at the lions.

One day a lion
took away a sheep.
David ran
after the lion.
God helped David,
and he brought
the sheep home.

One day a bear
took away a sheep.
David ran
after the bear.
God helped David,
and he brought
the sheep home.

One day
the Philistines
came to fight
the king's men.

The biggest Philistine
was a man named Goliath.
Goliath wanted to hurt
the king's men.

Goliath said,
"SEND SOMEBODY
OVER HERE
TO FIGHT ME."

The king
was afraid.
The king's men
were afraid.
Nobody said,
"I'll go."
And then,

David thought about the lion. *God helped me save the sheep.* David thought about the bear. *God helped me save the sheep.*

David thought
about Goliath.
Would God help David
save the king's men?
YES, HE WOULD.

So David was not afraid.
He said to the king,
"I will fight this man.
God will help me."

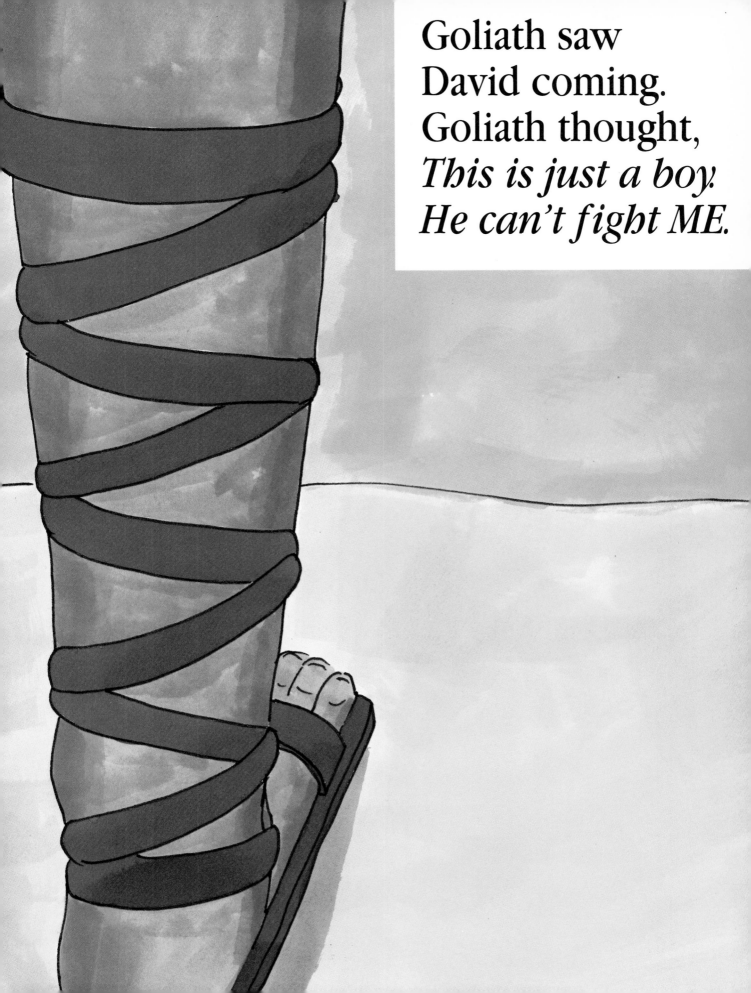

Goliath saw
David coming.
Goliath thought,
*This is just a boy.
He can't fight ME.*

But David said,
"You think
you are strong.
God is stronger.
He will help me."
And God did.

Round, round went David's sling.
Zip, zip went David's stone.

Down, down went Goliath.
All the Philistines ran away.
And David went to see the king.

What did you learn?

David was not afraid.
He knew he had a helper.
David's helper was God.
YOU don't need to be afraid.
You have a helper too.
Your helper is ___ (God).

Jonah and the Big Fish
(Jonah 1; 2)

Jonah was not happy.
Jonah said,
"I don't want to do
what God says.
I will run away."

*Step, step,
step, step,*
Jonah hurried
down the road.
Jonah got on a boat.
Away went the boat
on the blue water.
God saw Jonah go.
God knew
what Jonah needed.

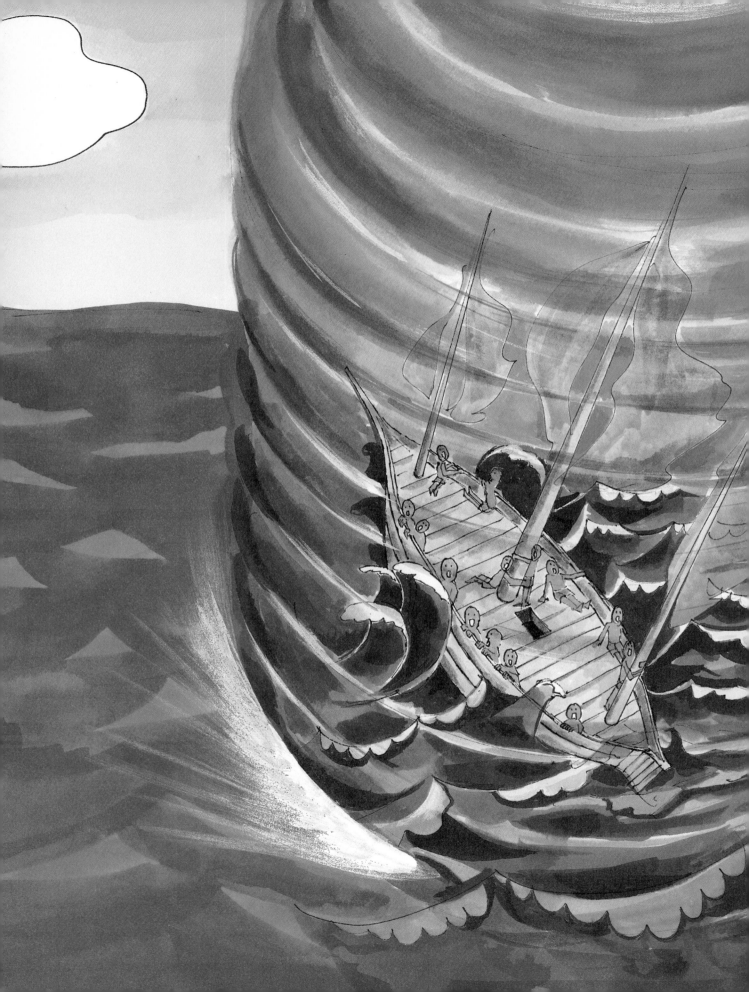

So God sent
a big wind
to help him.
Who-o-o.
God's wind blew
on the water.
Who-o-o.
God's wind blew
at the boat.
Who-o-o.
The water went
SPLASH!
Everybody got wet.

The men worked hard
to make the boat go.
But it wouldn't.
The men were afraid.
They said,

"SOMEBODY has done something wrong. That is why this big wind is trying to upset our boat. WHO IS IT?"

Then Jonah said,
"I did it.
I was trying
to run away
from God.
Just throw me
into the water.
Then the wind
will stop."

The men worked hard
to make the boat go.
But it wouldn't.
So they did
what Jonah said.
They picked him up.
They threw him
into the water.
SPLASH!
And then—

the wind did stop going
who-o-o, who-o-o.
The water did stop going
splash, splash.
The big storm went away
—all of it.

Now God knew
what Jonah needed.
God sent a big fish
to help him.
The big fish
opened its mouth—
WIDE.
It gobbled up Jonah
in ONE BITE!
Oh, my.
Did *that* help Jonah?
Yes, it did.

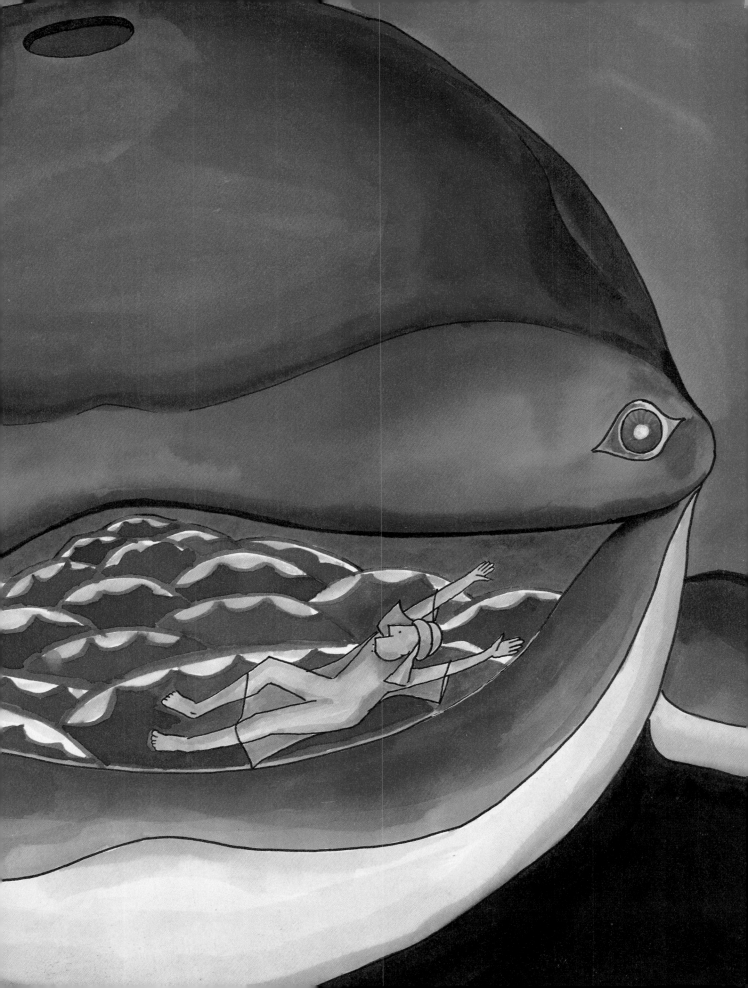

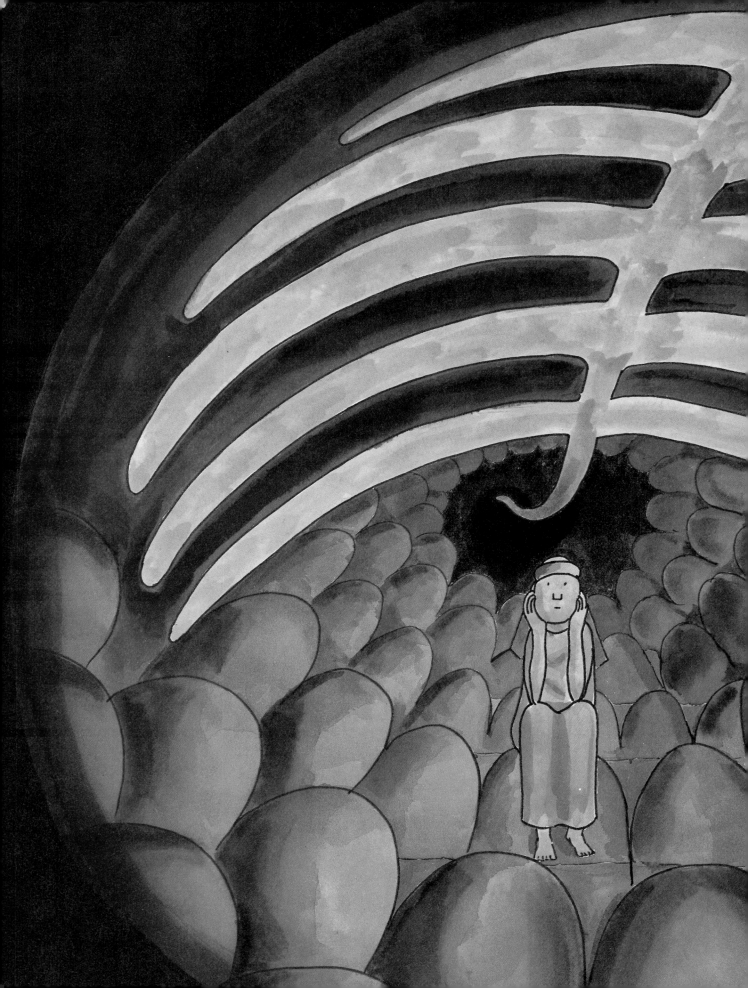

The next thing
Jonah knew,
there he sat
safe inside
the big fish.
It was dark.
It was wet.
Jonah didn't like it
in there.
But Jonah was safe.

Down, down, down
went the fish.
Down, down, down
went Jonah.
Then Jonah
talked to God.
"Help me, Lord,
and I will do
what You told me
to do."

Now God knew
what Jonah needed.
God told the fish,
"TAKE JONAH BACK
TO THE LAND."
The fish did
what God said.
After a while
it opened its mouth—
WIDE.

And the next thing
Jonah knew,
there he sat
on the nice dry sand.

Jonah stood up.
He looked around.
He saw the blue sky.
He saw the sunshine.
He saw the trees.
He thanked God.
And then—

Jonah went
*step, step,
step, step*
up the road
to do what God
told him.

What did you learn?

God knew what Jonah needed.
He sent the big wind to help.
God knew what Jonah needed.
He sent the big fish to help.
God knows what you need.
He wants to help you too.